BROADWAY 2

BROADWAY 2

A Poets and Painters Anthology

Edited by James Schuyler and Charles North

Hanging Loose Press

Published by Hanging Loose Press
231 Wyckoff Street
Brooklyn, New York 11217

Cover and design by Trevor Winkfield

Library of Congress Cataloging-in-Publication Data

Broadway 2 / edited by Charles North and James Schuyler.
    p. cm.
    ISBN 0-914610-71-6 :   — ISBN 0-914610-70-8 (pbk.)
      1. American poetry—20th century.   I. North, Charles. II. Schuyler, James.
III. Title: Broadway two.
PS615.B66   1989
811'.5408—dc20   89-7595
                                                       CIP

Produced at The Print Center., Inc., 225 Varick St., New York, NY 10014, a non-profit facility for literary and arts-related publications. (212) 206-8465

TABLE OF CONTENTS

BROADWAY 2

John Ash

The Sweeping Gesture

                              in the sky
was final above the hospital that was the colour of bread.

Emptiness like a permanent echo
remained in the streets, although the ghosts
of punks and panhandlers still hovered
in the improvised bazaars, stepping between photographs
of limbs splayed and bronzed, or torsos
uniformly 'god-like' in repose.

The scene was 'classic'. The question arose:
"If the people in the city dress as if
for the beach, what do they wear at the beach?
What pleasure is there in continual freedom from restraints?"
The grid is dropped over all colours and complaints,
and assigns to each its portion and locale. The wind lifts
the trash a little way to where the sun sears the rose leaves,
and a hand reaches for the warm drink that was cool a moment ago,—

O air, for some weeks absent from these shores!...

It is too early to leave and far beyond the point
when departure would have made a difference. You
sigh at this but continue packing anyway:

"on the island there are trees, and above the trees
are houses open to the slightest movement of the air,
and red-winged birds come to rest
on the weathered railings of their decks;
under the trees tunnels run from the ocean to the bay,
and all day we can see what comes and goes away.
Only, over Babylon, a dull cloud hangs."

So much for letters home (the kind that are never sent).
There must be more to it than heaven or hell, our dirt and their purity,
something that could stand contradiction without collapsing in a frenzy,
but you are already more cool and distant than a waterfall,—
you were never here, never belonged in these streets and avenues
where a single tree's survival seems a miracle. And they

are here in thousands,—
the planes, the maples, the gingkos, the honey-locusts
veiling the high cornices of our 'rusticated' tenements,
the smiling capitals of wealthy houses.

All the other places that come to mind,—
possible locations of other lives that might have been ours
with a change of luck—are neither exotic nor blessed:
they too are a part of what we call *home*,—
towers and bridges, wild flowers, boulevards,
mountains and demolished smokestacks,
and however far away the singer may be the song still arrives
with news from the hotel of the red quilt a mother stitched with stars.

It is time for these things to be part of understanding,
for mere opinion and impotent rage to diminish
to a murmur, a background harmony like the sob
of an off-stage horn, time for the art of illumination
to be revived in golden air. Already the small, blue
ferryboat puts out from the dock towards home or the city.

Minutes of silence are observed with every dawn,
and the buildings grow taller with the news of each loss.

John Ashbery

A Mourning Forbidding Valediction

And who, when all is said and done,
Cares for thee like me? I know. *Thy* name
Is known to me, and if thou sufferest like a squall
That sirens rend, I'll be confident and of the other
Persuasion. Perfume that drenches like a pall
Is the old scent, and dear, true; its fame
Waxeth with the sun
And is not like, moreover, a lost brother.

When glory's steed pawed the ground,
Frozen and flinty the hour, yet for some
It was command out of the deepest basin, and who shall say
Which recombinant molecules have memorized the next rote
And when the reciters have fall'n, on a day
Stuck in time's craw, that merriment is a crumb
Unfit for sharing, only a sound
Like itself, endless fishy smell or zygote.

Nothing's here; the year
Is ripe, and frozen, all about me stand
Censors—veiled, tumescent husks who at the last
Come clean in the moulting of the season, and make no bones
About their city of origin. Them too, held fast
In memory's drizzle, the Place St. Ferdinand
Negates, and surrounding highrises, mere
Chaff, or the power which breeds stones

And shall have much to say, come night-
Fall, and all around us awful blisters concur
In melting trusses, stalk the errant ptarmigan
Or deed no entry to fools and nimble savants beyond the moat
That weeps for times when the green cardigan
Of duckweed shrouded it, and, all exemplary, her
Nose protruded beyond the outline of the bight
Some saw beyond, and her raincoat.

To scrape the habit from our stand of being, and, once
It's accomplished, rescue it from shyness, out of a burrow
Of pleasure up toward greater mounds of pleasure, is to a name
What places are, and so be it
If trace elements are added and rules from the game
Subtracted little by little. Ergo,
Someone's won it. Dunce
Am I? So's your old man, you stupid shit.

Gallons and gallons of water slid over the weir
But since it was night, no one knew or cared. The owl
For all its feathers was a-cold. Peace lay in sections
On the raised edge of a circus ring, where sawdust
Conjures belly's emptiness and the recent elections
Are commented. Men prowl
Beside the recently abandoned pier
Sprung from any concept, from reckonings, crust

Of someone else's negligence, our cognizance.
O skate too far away, or else backpack, backtrack
Into the hay of an argument dimly seen, unscathed
Like time. The more marbles to our monument
The more the future won't be any less real to us, enswathed
In Hyperborean conundrums—that's as may be. To bushwhack
From here to Petaluma, then chance
Failed irrigation canals, faults, is my soul's sole integument.

Susan Baran

Harmonious Whole

Fire levels, what goes down
goes up again.
Fear, incense of ashes,
the unholy hills, and opportunity,
a whole city begging to be recast.

And I was there fresh
from Beaux Arts in Paris,
full of the sustaining past.
A tiny woman, bird-like
they called me. It did not matter—

I knew stone cutters, masons,
glaziers. I knew direction,
purpose, how to coax
my vision from empty air.
They wanted magic, amnesia

To free them from the licking flames.
My hotel rose above the mists
of Avalon, a crown on the crystal bay
grand as any palace of Europe.
Some snickered—I was aware

But did not falter.
After the Fairmont there were offers,
the whole of California
hungry for a scheme.
I did as much as God

Gave me time or strength for—
Hacienda del Pozo del Verona,
Examiners buildings, whatever.
That was how I met him,
he was tired of going

Up there and camping in tents.
A simple plan—a single structure
of the kind known as a bungalow.
Three weeks into it his eyes
began to dance, the word

Regal whispered.
It tore at my heart—
All the rest preliminary.
He had resources
and that brazen fiefdom

By the sea. We would
pierce the star-riddled sky.
Still, we were cautious
by future standards,
sought to charm by detail

Rather than overwhelm
by clumsy exuberance.
Workmen were reluctant
to come to such desolation.
The chef was the most

Important man on the mountain.
The output of the kilns
came in spoonfuls,
some of it lovely
in color. The big pour,

1923, Casa Grande.
He sent—I sorted, absorbed,
cabled back, "finer
and more important things
would be welcome."

Bill Berkson

Way How

Markets hit return
the egregious debauch
and in the garden

ever remotely broken car:
contempt city at the bypass
creasing good-natured binges.

The layouts of minus
squat on the rooftops
of princely Eden.

Wet jewels waxing into struts,
thankful factory scraps,
hot potions brought in on trays —

the way it sounds at this end.

Charles Bernstein

Autonomy Is Jeopardy

I hate artifice. All these
contraptions so many barriers
against what otherwise can't
be contested, so much seeming
sameness in a jello of
squirms. Poetry scares me. I
mean its virtual (or ventriloquized)
anonymity—no protection, no
bulwark to accompany its pervasive
purposivelessness, its accretive
acceleration into what may or
may not swell. Eyes demand
counting, the nowhere seen everywhere
behaved voicelessness everyone is clawing
to get a piece of. Shudder
all you want it won't
make it come any faster,
last any longer: the pump
that cannot be dumped.

Jim Brodey

Some Recent News From The Frontier

". . .a textbook punch"

—*Alan Bernheimer*

Feelings are more like pictures
Of something I can feel and know
But not explain and rather see

Like Pasternak when his students came
To ask his permission to sign the letter
That would imprison him in his own home

Boris looked at them sadly as they walked
Into the woods beyond his gate "Now" he sd
"They will never be able to have a future

In poetry" and I am wondering as tears
Run down my cheeks which of the graves
I have dug for myself I will actually use

The flowers look radiant and new
Are the colors of the sky but
Its exactly the same sky he once saw

And we both understood the nature of careers
As I read so shall I learn to discover
Patience in the signs on this trail & how

To continue to be able to write of them
Information must be made softer rather than
High and I am not telling you anything

He did not know but knowing is not always
Understanding and frequently I feel it
But cannot say it in the same way color

Has an edge to it and we are lost in effect
By reading I try to rekindle my flame to
Which we all verge to urge ourselves forward

Reading it is not the same as living through
The cold flames of life's interruptions &
I know I knew him once in my own flesh but

Now I can only see him on the page and when
He comes to me it is without breath & I
I'm not that same person in this impersonal dream

I hold my hands out to you Boris & the dream
That was our breath turned to flames come
Roaring back to my eyes that have the color

Of these words I seek to tell
We struggle with these things
Against the mercy of grammatical wolves

Where once I swam in words' fury
The furious deaths mount to a hill
Of invisible beans & I swim in poems

Never to be dry again & the flames
Came and the bodies filled up morning
Where those flowers had no faces

The Russian tongue is a difficult music
As the Polish tongue is a beautiful song
And the cats in heaven know this music

They are laughing & their breathing
Obliterates any page you think they'll
Stay put upon yes its crazy and yes

We're willing to ride this craziness
For we have no choice but to submerge
Bodies in their own music

When Boris died I felt the stir as of old
And blood rose to my eyes and my heart
Took up music's revolver aiming it

Straight into blinding light
When cities boil in their breathing
And white filth sweeps this plain

We shall regain the rosy crown of language
Connecting primary colors to this sky
As refreshment is made available so I

Swear to keep your heart beating
Against the lesser of a million furies
Who I shall be and always remain

7-7-88

Donna Brook

WIPPSI

The never-changing wet mess of birth, of coupling, living
in this hamster-on-its-wheel metropolis because of heterosexual love
with a new cruel knowledge of family life each secret
hanging in the window of a Chinese restaurant like a duck,
and this. . .this man
who rubs Avocado Body Lotion into my back
comes home, reaches into the ice cubes,
pours the Scotch, doesn't seem to know
what the hell I do for a living

"Michael," he tells me, "had to go to a special testing center for standardized tests that
all the private schools require for kindergarten. Isn't that amazing?" "No."

Many, many Monday afternoons of
looking at scores on an overhead projector plus
a month of workshops describing each subtest
of the WIPPSI in detail also
every year I give a full set of ERBs to ten year olds who
cry each year if a child's
performance score on the Vocabulary Subtest is at
great variance with her score on the Comprehension we assume
she is experiencing a high level of anxiety but if another little girl
at another school arrives dirty and covered with bruises nobody seems
to assume a damn thing

Suppose, when he was working on Animal House, Michael tried to fit the sheep into
the cow space? Suppose he got lost in Mazes, dizzy in Geometric Design, inappropriate
during Vocabulary? What if in Picture Completion he finally painted that space Gilbert
Stuart left around Washington? What if, in Similarities, he said that the Elizabethans
called orgasm dying because he'd heard that at home? Yet Arithmetic would never be
a problem. Everyone in New York City knows what adds up. I teach what adds up to
those who added up well. And if, in the Information Subtest, when he was asked,
"What do you need if it rains," Michael said, "an umbrella," he'd be judged fine but
average. If he said, "a big boat with two of every kind of animal," no one would know

if he were well-informed or terrified. These tests are not easy to interpret. People must be trained to administer and decipher them. The scores do not have visible results like black-and-blue marks.

maybe it's because it's sentimental Xmastime
that I'm so aware of who is a child and who shouldn't be
but all that rain-forest August
Charles and Paula wouldn't close their bedroom door
to run the air-conditioning unit
so that they could hear Michael sleep

December 1988

Dear Sarge

I can't remember the politics.
All I know is day's light
and night is dark.
I think of facing north on Folsom
at Arapahoe, and the being renovated
gas station with the orange
plastic keep-out fence
dark under streetlights with
carlights and the Folsom Grill in neon.
I spread out in day, close up at night.
Sarge, generally speaking, do you
think that most of the country
believes in God? Do you think they feel
the same about who He is?
Would they like to be Him
or do they like being Him or do they
want to be His friend, His children?
Sarge, what about the words of Blake
"a fibre from the Brain does tear"?
A fibre of the Brain, what does it
feel like, Sarge, when it tears? The same
for you as me?

That stretched-out orange keep-out fence
the wind can pass through, stretches
with what it can hold.
All that comes through
the holes in the fence of our senses
comes through as tension, Sarge
as tension.

A laser cuts shapes in steel belts.
It saws frictionlessly through the
melted wires, interrupting the tension
we took for granted, making us know
a little bit about being gone.
Our muscles,
especially the ones in back,
are continually flashing this tension
we feel but don't know. Sarge
sometimes these muscles
tear, ripped by the tension
in the atmosphere.
When the sun lands on the horizon
it gets jelly-like and smooth
like a living organ, when it
lifts onto the plains, swelling
before it goes up high.
The sun is a homeless man in the street
Sarge. Can you imagine that?
The sun is a homeless man in the street?
Well, that's what happened, just now
that's what I imagined. Sarge
do you think that's the end
or the beginning
of the poem

Poem

The mountains, red
Wave upon wave, stop at
A row of palms
Where my grandmother once
Lived and died.
You are here, dark and lovely,
Jesus of the Palms;
Jesus of the Mountains.
Behind you, the blue ocean
Wrapped in yellow and white. I
Kiss your hands and feet.
I am your brother Thomas:
Child of this ocean, these
Mountains; there is
Blood in my mouth.

9/11/88

What It's Like

The squirrel leaping frightens
the pigeon walking over you

In this return of winter,
snow on branches,
in this ravine of sorrow.

A bird's wings like a
heart beats
over adrenaline snow,
yet I know you're not here.

There's no sound
not even the silence
broken by a gun,

not even of the thunder
of drugged eyes,

not even of ecstasy
half asleep in the breast,

Yet I know the bare feet
of narrow salvation

in the dirt and dust around us
follows all day.

In the same way a light breaks
into a coal mine

do I explode all the fantasy
of description and metaphor

and leave with a blush, in snow

Leap Year Day

The paleolithic heart might burst
with news of slowness, news of feathers.
All the softness listed in the register
you keep: day of finite crashing.
Who's to say the deafness that you wore
was needed by the Greeks? Depression
sounded like a whole note sewn with
lilac thread. I wanted to assure you
that the small biology of kissing
would not last until the last pebble dried
and a flag wobbled and a list faded and a map
was drawn and a green planet drifted
under your lens. The elbowed dawn lifted,
and you said nothing of the storm that flashed
off-shore, as if to mean, forgotten winter
without signs. You will not fade.
I believe your wholeness as it rests its future
on our lengthening half-lit letters.

Marc Cohen

At The Precipice

This is a shocking poem that might be
hazardous to your health, or could harbor
disaster, because the possibility
of its success had never been thought of—
most American towns don't even have a cliff
that is steep enough to jump from,
but right here there is a rock face
that is almost vertical, and represents
a true point of danger.
It is up to you, the reader,
to make certain that this can never happen again.
Please burn this poem after you have read it—
you can't expect me to do that,
I, like you, need something to live for.

Let's go back a little further though,
but not to a place in the sun or a dark passage.
Actually, it begins here on this page,
in this particular room or stanza.
I'm not sure how all of this trouble got started,
but once it started there was a snowball effect.
I know it could never happen again
in a million years, or at least until tomorrow.
What confuses you, also confuses me.
As soon as I clean up the mess,
I can't wait for things to get out of place again—
I find it hard to wait for the chaos to work
its way through me, or for me to be able
to shout back at the deafening silence.

Maybe I could have stopped them,
but once they convinced me of the virtues
of their plan, I was just along for the ride.
Their expressions at that fateful moment before,

stay with me as if I had photographed them
at the precise moment and kept the photograph
on the mantel or in my wallet.
Their sadness transformed me,
made me ralize that it is necessary to be aware
of the small print, and that you can only hope
for happiness. If I hadn't understood,
they wouldn't have been able to sanctify
or stamp my approval. To reason things out,
is not always the most practical way of proceeding,
sometimes a bold, ignorant action must be taken.

So it ended on this page, dear reader,
and like the strong arm of the law
chasing down the murderer who is also the victim,
the emotions that had been put on ice and quelled,
were off and running wild like the dogs
that were used to track the footprints
that mysteriously formed a circle,
not knowing whether to ask for our return,
or tell us to leave the town for good,
translating both your original desire and mine
into a new version of wanted dead or alive.

Glance In White Space

No detail here, nothing but you. Unbroken gaze,
whole of the body, words cast away. It is level with
meaning, this white horizon. And when the air comes
together we bend.

Little strokes. The air has parted many. That the
perking lights all are you. And the time is a favor
presented to no one. Previously, whole.

Gone out like a wish, forgotten spoken. Dividing line
each touch. Novels could be ignored, or spent
in this chamber.

Little more than you telling me, with a brightness here
or now. Beneath skin, where the flesh begins.
Our clothing an imitation, a skin to remove.

Blush of red soak on the glass, into itself.
On the morning the unknown colors start, and the ones
we know imprisoned change.

Enclosing wind, air in lace chains. Torn flowers,
bronzed hedgerows, the moon as cut a sign.
The you I will be before you.

Whatever

Whatever's
to be
thought
of thinking
thinking's
thought of
it still
thinks
it thinks
to know
itself so
thought.

Thought so
itself know to
thinks it
thinks still it
of thought
thinking's
thinking
of thought
be to
whatever's.

Spoof's Cabaret Song
(from "Night Emerald",
an opera libretto based on the life of Oscar Wilde)

FOUR TOFFS: In every strand, every square,
There's a decadent air.
Every toff longs to chafe
For a handsome young waif.

It's the newest of fads.
Gents are loony for lads.
Every rake has an ache
For a tyke on the make.

FOUR RENTERS: Ow's about a light, sir?
Ow's about a smoke?
Pinin' for a mite, sir?
Starvin' for a bloke?
Care to pass the night, sir?
Care to share a pint?
You're a bleedin' s'int, sir—
I'm so famished, I could f'int.

FOUR TOFFS: In every rococo pile
Where there's nary a smile,
Every blade is aflame
For The Love With No Name.

It's the oldest of yens,
Chasing roosters, not hens.
With a chap on one's lap,
Joie de vivre's a snap.

1ST TOFF: I gave up my mistresses, my greyhounds and my pipe,
For the love of a too-too utterly utter guttersnipe.

FOUR TOFFS: Decrepid duffers with gout
Who once tottered about
Now go waltzing with chums
Commandeered in queer slums.

It's the newest of fads.
Gents are loony for lads.
Ganymede wearing tweed
Is seductive indeed.

2ND TOFF: A tryst with an Adonis is uplifting, if he's pristine.
3RD TOFF: And resembles Adam on that ceiling in the Sistine.
4TH TOFF: Chasing classic nymphs is out of fashion—too Philistine.
FOUR RENTERS: Why dally with a floozy, luv?
Buggers can be choosy, luv.

FOUR TOFFS: In London Town, every park
Brightens up after dark,
And the smart hoi polloi
Spurn the tart, snatch the boy.

Guardsmen and bootblacks,
Chimneysweeps and drummers,
Grooms and valets
Fan the blaze of golden summers,

Poshest of trends.
Lavender friends.
Wing starry-eyed.
Spring to our stride.
Chap on one's lap.
Vivre's a snap.
Newest of fads.
Lads.

Words Read By Lightning

Big silver raucous stem
solemn rippling it was

nearly eleven
when we arrived
and the combination
of the storm
and the scotch
had made everyone giddy

except us.

There was one opera
in the air
and a different one
on the air

and that impressed me

as well as
the delicate manner
in which people
disposed of their garbage
carrying it
from curb to curb
as if to make it
more comfortable.

This then was a place
where many vicarious
pleasures gathered

the wood
from which I'd make
my legs

where one could lead
a thousand lives
without lifting
a finger

the hands
already full
with what is.

In One Sentence

In one sentence what is the story of your life. I've been knifed. It's all in the wrist, or ghost. Effect comes first, you leave before you arrive. You gotta be massless to keep up the pace. Twisted tchaikowsky.

*   *   *

Groping, you miss the first few words: "lit from within." Keys to the meaning of sacred scenes vanished when you were growing up. A cop car driving right through a guy's legs. Women being drained of their blood, emptying into the street like the audience. Now if you want to see a beautiful scene look at the window: curtains made of comic strips pasted on unbleached muslin with borders of scotch tape. Isn't that something. Carefully he put his creation inside his camera. More light on the wall, shot with the heart. Through a glass ashtray, cut with the head. I see coffee drunk by a green hand. I see Jean Seberg sitting up dead in Paris. I see people having their being. I see white lines on a sullen sea. Eyeless shrimp, the faint light at the ocean floor. I wish I had more eyes.

*   *   *

She walks in beauty by the bank, a girl just back from France. He gets her a job singing in a spot of his, she is of course sensational. But ixnay see because in walks the opposition mob leader. Plots, alarms, the gathering of the clans. Generals without buttons, golf without clubs or balls, all drowned out by bagpipes. A movie so sodden one could barely rise to go damply, limply home.

*   *   *

How do you explain school to a higher intelligence? I was a Romper Room reject (light tap on the rear with a ruler). First I understood nothing but the beauty which came to me in books. If I jump into a flame I'm liable to cool off. What does my *finger* remember? Shrouds of dragonflies struggling free. A hole in the knee. Got my ears lowered, won't have to bend down. Looking at a pussy. Putting up your poems.

Bumps on the head by venomous tuskahorian gazonian blengin. Fire the retro rocket, Mister Bodylegs. In the foundling hospital they took away my beeper. Wasn't Alexander working on a never-ending life tool? Turtles are eternal, pirates are undressing ladies. I'm rubber, you're glue, anything you say. When is it over. Ever. So much of the old heaven and the old earth has passed away, a whole new generation can't be traced. A clock that ticks only when it wants to, the time-life removal. What is the meaning of happen. Bread and jam in the dirt. Why don't people who take nitroglycerine for a heart condition explode?

Mary Ferrari

The Vocation

I have an irritable heart with a floppy valve, like a rusty hinge on a gate. My doctor says it is difficult to cure infections in an irritable heart.

It is difficult to keep sitting alone at a table in the middle of this tiny French restaurant, "Tout Va Bien." I've been waiting for my husband for a half-hour, and growing larger, my heart growing more irritable, where is he?

He was robbed and has just been murdered by thieves.

I lift up my irritable heart unto the world, higher than skyscrapers and stars! I also let it fall lower than subways and sewers! This way everyone now alive will some day pass through the rusty gate of my irritable heart.

Smiling and serene, my husband arrives.

It is his birthday! Tout va bien.

Ed Friedman

What Is Semiotics?

for Tony Towle

Wake up take bath
Breeze blows in on my sweaty back
Listen to Lori make beeps with the Donkey Kong
Take Pepsi empties to the store for deposits

Such is the problem of *identity*
What then is *struggle*?

Bob Holman's country house in Pennsylvania
Bob Rosenthal's country home in Wisconsin
Bob Kushner's country home in Warwick

I have no country home
Clearly Ed Bowes & I have the wrong first names

Monkey's seventy-two metamorphoses are more to the point
Anne sez "Has Bernadette talked to you yet?"
I say "No. Is there something she's supposed to tell me?"
"Yes, she has become heaven's warbler of truth on this earth full of countless
    directives and practicalities on our next 20 years of great leaps forward and back
    as frogs on lilies whose sweetness can barely be known in this lifetime. . ."
"Or in one careless instant," I say.
"A -true a-true," sez Anne,
"And aren't we ashamed of ourselves for thinking dinky."

Here's my 20-year plan:

Wake up roll over play dead
Be thinner rise to power
Caress 20 fascinating lovelies and have Lori not be jealous
Bowl 300 change my underwear
And lie down

With the people on all sides of me
Singing with great abandon
Poems from the Nomadic System of Mongolia
Spellbinding and with great heartbreak
Their hand motions
A universal tongue

Allen Ginsberg

May Days 1988

As I cross my kitchen floor the thought of Death returns,
day after day, as I wake & drink lemon juice & hot water,
brush my teeth & blow my nose, stand at toilet a yellow stream
issuing from my body, look out curtained windows, across the street
Mary Help of Christians R.C. Church, how many years
empty the garbage pail, carry black plastic bags to the sidewalk,
before I boil the last soft egg,
day after day glance my altar sitting pillow a sidelong look & sigh,
Pass bookcases' greek lyrics unread & volumes of Military Industrial Secrecy—
How many mornings out the window Springtime's grey clouds drift over a
   wooden owl
on the Rectory roof, pigeons flutter off the street lamp to an iron fence, I return to
   kitchen
oatmeal cooking in an iron pot, sit in a wooden chair, choose a soupspoon,
   dreaming out the window eat my gruel
as ailanthus trees bud & grow thick green, seaweed in rainy Atlantis,
lose leaves after Snowfall, sit bare branched in January's rusty winds?
Snap photographs focus'd on the clothesline, courtyard chimmeypots a block
   away?
How many years lie alone in bed and stroke my cock
or read the Times on a pillow midnite, answer telephone talk, my Stepmother
or Joe in Washington, wait for a knock on the door it's portly Peter sober   hesitant
inquiring supper, rarely visiting, rueful a life gone by—you got the monthly rent?
armfuls of mid-morn mail arriving with despairing Secretaries—
rise and tuck my shirt in, turn the doorlock key, go down hallway stairs
enter New York City, Christine's Polish restaurant around East 12th Street corner
   on 1st Avenue
taxi uptown to art museums or visit Dr. Brown, chest x rays, smoking cough or flu
Turn on the News from Palestine, Listen to Leadbelly's lament on tape, *Black Girl,*
   Jim Crow, Irene—and
Sunday Puerto Ricans climb concrete steps week after week to church.

May 1, 1988 Noon

II

Sox in the laundry, snap on the kitchen light midnite icebox
raid, sun dried tomatos soft swiss cheese & ham, Pineapple juice,
low rent control $260 per mo, clear gymseal sanded-floors, white walls,
Blake's *Tyger* on the bedroom bookcase, cabs rattling on dark asphalt below,
Silence, a solitary house, Charles Fourier on bedside table waiting inspection,
reading glasses ready with neck string to hang on my breast if I rise, switch light
    off—
Pyjamas in drawer for sleep, 80 volumes behind the headboard for browsing
Yiddish Poetry, Atilla Josef, Das Gupta's *Obscure Religious Cults*, Céline, De
    Vulgaria Eloquentia—
What riches for old age? What cosy naps and long nights dreams? Browsing in
    Persepolis and Lhasa!
What more ask existence? Except time, more time, ripe time & calm,
& Warless time to contemplate collapsing years, tho body teeth & brain and elbow
    ache,
a crooked creak at backbone bottom, dry nostrils, mottled ankle
& smart tongue, how many years to talk, snap photos, sing in theaters
improvise in classroom street, church & radio, far from Congress.
How many more years eyes closed at 9 AM wake worrying
the ulcer in my cheek is't cancer? Should I have charged Burroughs' biographer for
    photos
reprinted from 40 years ago? Miles the editor's stylistic competence OK
for Lit Hist Beat Generation? Should I rise & meditate
or sleep in daylight recuperate flu? phone ringing half an hour ago
What's on the Answer Machine? Give back Advances to Harpers?
Who promised deadlines for this photo book? Wasn't I up 2 AM revising Poems?
Spontaneous verse?!? Take a plane to Greenland, visit Dublin?
Pen Club meet May 17, decision Israeli Censorship Arabic Press?
Call Cynthia Ozick yiddish translator poetess Zionist yenta?
write concentration camp expert moralist Eli Weizel, What's his word
"Arabs shd throw words not stones?" is that quote accurate from the Times?
Should I get up right now, crosslegged scribbling Journals
with motor roar downstairs in the street, stolen autos being doctor'd at the curb
or pull the covers over achy bones? How many years awake or sleepy
How many mornings to be or not to be?

How many morning Mays to Come, birds chirp mornings insistent on six story
    roofs?
buds rise in backyard cities? Forsythia yellow by brick walls & rusty bedsprings
    near the fence?

III

How many Sundays wake and lie immobile eyes closed remembering Death,
Get up at 7 AM Spring Sunlight out the window the noise a Nuyorican drunkard
    on the corner
remind me of Peter, Naomi, my nephew Alan, am I mad myself, have always been
    so
waking in NY 61st year to realize childless I am a motherless freak
like so many millions worlds from Paterson Los Angeles to the Amazon
Humans & Whales screaming in despair from Empire State Building top to Arctic
    Ocean bottom—?

Stem Time

       When the spark came
I was doing a gig
going to Rome like the song said, vision
intended my liberation
           over the river
where sight swam
And as it were
      amphibious, in the rose
in many of the coronary plants

           Am I blue?
put your nose to the mirror
I was that close, bosoms
        against
a panoramic hearing.   Her ass
shall not inter me
      I am old
So long
so Youth
   you are a state a remnant
of some wanna

Yeah,
   and all that booty
must smother thee

Mahler's 2nd

In the beginning was the worm and the worm
Turned to sod. It is the spring
That undoes winter which quilted is quiet
Light building in solitary progression.
One block of lead after the other moving
In an endless array of gray tho humorless
Is worn demurely which is the custom.

Only spring is listless myth. Myopic
Ecstasy with nether earth, for a keep sake
Is a rainy day a wishing well in afternoon.
A hand becoming an object portends a translation,
An artifact only dust will embrace intimately.
Say when does the phallus become a prick?

The river moves we are moved. This is
Not uncommon our momentary communion with
House, mountain, water is all ours to
Transcend as we arrive. This spring is
Chilled awakening to touch these tendons
Moving a darker reluctance into blossom.
Inescapable cant of the axis/heart.

Importunate Everlasting Attractions

On the line between gray and blue, Lincoln sits in his monument. Except for the blue and the gray, it is a long breeze from 12th Street. Upstairs I leave a car-fire view and march to the sea. Without, as they say, pudgy guys need money and the batteries fall out of her back before she can get into the car. For every darkened headlight in town there's a lawyer, and all over the city people constantly fall. I go on feeling this brown heat to which creatures bearing any hair at all contribute. So much villainy welcomed through so many doors, a source of endless enchantment to me. Bit by bit a tune has to expend more energy to remain part of the city night heights. I whistle "Lady Be Good" across to Third Avenue and the whoors put on their screwy looks. Black aprons in earth-colored rooms, and earth-colored legs ahead of me up the stairs. Climbing the vines, that's what I'm doing, and the high point in the jungle is probably a tit. I don't clown around when the bulb lights up on the wee dark streets. Here's to discharges, all kinds! Here's to preparations made ill by circumstances! And here's to me, kissing through the pullaway window as the yellow sedan heads out of the Borough of Pantyhose! I want a wave over me from time to time, to feel sophisticated.

Tell this to a little girl in cold rain. How coolness is as important a hub as the sun. Everything becomes eventually the temperature of the air. An example is diamonds, an example is guts. And some day I will increasingly be able to address her as "the late yourself." Cooling gives her face a great aura. Silver curves around all of hers. Silver chain in the hand of a god statue holding its dick? Moist or dry, but cool. The feet going numb in pursuit of the soul, which overexposes itself to tunnelled light. Black fog blows into the city avoiding its brights. Watching, I feel consonance. No vows whatsoever. Heart like a shiny bar of sand, a little bit of hate, a bit of disdain, and an injury I reject. If they don't hear me, they aren't alive. As long as they come and go without any splashing. A splash in a million on the lost avenue, where you need a witness to sign your "X."

GMT

You're the best at what you do
As you dream, inside the bed
Where ground is broken
And adulthood rises through slum
Clearance   The person
Becomes all door, painted for decor,
Whiff motives from island salons
You're the best at what you do
And I can't live with that
Because it's describing a fax
Tomorrow I will think of you
On the couch, in the kitchen
Of the second person
Cleaning up after at first

Barbara Guest

Emotive Waters

choose octagonals as chatter.

                                  smiles become

a passage   shallow

   glass changes.

                                 combs drop

and tease.

                   in scumbled flax

               a foreigness.   secret-filled

emotive waters

munition of

                   imminence.

                             lay on

       the cut marble

       sestina figured.

the wave that obeys

                        the supple. textured.

speed of water.

                      can take away.

How To Pet

Knowing when to stop is like eating a poodle
What you say after that is somewhat suspect
So why not eat the entire family.
Chewing on a pencil, look out the window, lost in thought.
Years fly by, I assure you, if you eat like this.
Sitting down to read a book, sinking into severe depression
Can't shake off the chill, no matter what.
Withdrawal symptoms from sugar and alcohol likely
Sitting around taking apart a perfect dinner party
Bringing into life what is already there
The icecubes glistening in the eyes of wolves.
That's how it is.
Sometimes, the gentlest parts are the saddest.
Dear so and so, will you and please melt the wax
For feeling the way I do, I can't help devouring the pets.
Stop. I know when to stop.

Gerrit Henry

If

If one is born too lonely to feel—
If there is an exacting correlation
Between the way we act
And the way they deal—

If no one really minds
(And no one should,
If often, they do)—
If I could sensibly love you—

If kindness is a farce
And joy a mutation—
If no one can say,
And having said that, turn away—

If you care for me now,
Despite luck and elation—
Not minding when or how,
As if the wind could smell snow—

If death has a face,
And that face is death—
And if you shouldn't pay any attention
To what the Lord hath saith—

If, where there is generosity,
There is still room to give—
If our twisted sympathies
Would just allow us to live—

As if Jerusalem were the kingdom
Of no turning back—
If what can be put in writing
Could be put into words—

If the sun is black
With a million birds—

If everything means something
Which cannot be known—
If you scan the horizon
For cloud or stone—

If the sky is swollen
From too much rain—
If most things happen
For more than gain—

What if the trees kneel,
Or if there is no new, dumb song?
What if I wait for you,
And wait too long?

If you love me,
Wear my heart on your sleeve—
But only if what you believe
Is truer than what you discover—

Only if there is time enough,
And if you'll stay and be my lover—

If you'll hang around
And rehearse with me
That heart's hieroglyph—
If.

Robert Hershon

The Shroud Of Turin

Here was a woman's refrigerator upon the side of which
if you were standing at the proper angle the face of
Jesus could be seen clearly unless her neighbor
turned off his porch light
                                but cars clogged the street
for blocks around anyway, anything to avoid the inevitability
of automatic ice-making and if it were really an American miracle
she might sell a few cold sodas and beers

What other opportunities should she explore? Well,
I am on the mailing list of the Minister-by-Mail in Georgia who
sends me an 11x17 poster reproducing the Shroud of Turin
on 60-lb. white offset stock, printed black and one PMS color,
and on the other side appears a Prayer Rug with two ovals
knocking out white and marked Place Left Knee Here Place
Right Knee Here and if you send the Minister-by-Mail
some money he wants you to return the poster to him
so others may benefit from this blessing
                                        But I kept mine
I was going to hang it up on the wall but I couldn't
make up my mind which side I would show the world and
which side would be mine, alone

                                The shroud remains a hot
ticket even if carbon dating proves it's a fourteenth century
fraud   That, Cardinal Ballestrero says,
should not prevent the faithful from coming to the shrine
to requisition miracles   Beware of imitation imitators, he warns
Just be patient, stay in line, maintain silence, the doors
will open soon   It's very warm in here which is
how we imagine it's cold out there

The Story

The story had a thousand tattoos:
madonnas, sailing ships, serpents with tongues of flame,
and LOVE and HATE on the backs of its fingers.
There was also a pastoral scene
like the stained glass windows of churches.
A tough-looking Jesus Christ
looked up at the shoulder blades
(where two blue angels were painted),
and next to that, on the story's side,
a smoking train entered a tunnel.
But the story was normal enough.
It worked in a service station,
and on the weekends it ruled some little country
with "ia" on the end.
The real story, though, was the story's daughter,
who wound up running U.S. Steel
whenever she wore carnations—
something like that anyway.
She remembered her parent fondly,
for there was only one,
and it bore her out of its forehead one April afternoon,
on a day very much like this.

Alan Dunn

Vincent Katz

Temptation   8/8/88

New York is awash in urine.
But it's my head, can't escape
harpsichord rain, it's Friday
off Wooster Willem Dafoe looms
out of the dark, our eyes lock
later I realize tonight is "Last Temptation
of Christ" premiere, why he had
that look, my only poem of the summer,
almost over, why—pasting poems
in book, hearing old tape I'd made
"Lighter Shade" thought of Lennon
dead while pasting Alice's poem
of "labial delicacies…puckery poppies"
and her losing Ted—why this strange
combination? I'm not morbid really
but look! Jean-Michel Basquiat just 27 it's Tuesday
ugh, it's 5! Why do I always stay up
till 5? then have to stoke myself
with coffee to get to work, in sun at least
it's summer, despite "third hottest summer
since 1869," despite dank urine stench,
despite, despite, it's summer, it's hot, it's not cold,
there's sun, and anyway the light is
so clear at this hour, actually six.

Looking through old stuff: throwing out and saving,
Letter from Gerard Malanga (1979): coincidences, Dante, poetry, history,
then tape from then turns to Velvet sweet Jane version with
               "Wine and roses seem to
               whisper to me
               when you smile"
$5 Christmas gift from grandparents c. 1980 never used!
Who's Andrew G. Carrigan? I like what's in his poem:
tits, sidewalk cafe, t-shirt in Paris, wine glass, sun, wet nipples

Always something trite and yielding goes
with the heavy levelling—there, as a joke,
almost. Saccharine canned trash, she
slams receiver down, fat bulk exit.

So a perfect five-inch-high floortable:
eight years after finding on street returns
to street again: I leave fantastic gifts:
Mexican mask, wooden huge salad forks...
but it's natural. Throwing those old
love letters out too. Old love has
one meaning: no meaning. (In *those*
letters, others I keep...)
I want to write everything down,
so I don't forget it.

I was recently relieved of another fallacy:
that everybody is a great artist. Young, burning
they all seem so. She is waiting, at home
in bed for him, and he can imagine her
there, exactly as he is now on the street
she is there. She pushes down with
innuendo on my cock that is rising up.
I put my head on your back, where you are lying.
It is scary to write poems that have never been written.

Why did I write? the numbers came
and the girls, and everything: it feels
so good. With foresight, he says, "I will possess
everything, for I want nothing."
I wear my styles as a sign,
that others may know what I were.

8/8/88
9/20/88

Kenneth Koch

Homage To Frank O'Hara

HOMAGE TO FRANK O'HARA

Sometimes it seems to me I am possessed by the
spirit of Frank O'Hara and should write his poems
as he would have written them now but
the only ones I know are ones he's already written
and those are what these turn out to be. Oh
well! there should be more of Frank O'Hara
written at any time! Even if his are
better, why not have some of these? And I can
at least add subjects—the decease
of the Williamsburg Bridge might
have inspired him. Williams! What ever got into your steel
supports? How am I going
to get to Brooklyn to see
the nineteenth-century American
drawings at the Brooklyn Museum if you won't
lift me? Remember you're named for William
Carlos Williams and he didn't just
write a few poems and collapse, did he? No! Get up!

TO FRANK 2

Junk Junk Junk and I read in the paper that
they have gotten more than four million
for a Pollock oh well he deserves it somebody
deserves it he is dead and Lee deserves it
and Ruth deserves it she will
probably never get it does
she deserve it? I don't know. I am in favor
of giving part of it to her and the rest, say

three million and a half
dollars—Ruth! don't be angry like a rocky futon!—for
buying new crash-proof
cars for painters, so they can live
for ever! I'm eating
breakfast and it's already late.

TO FRANK O'HARA WITH MY INSPIRATION DIMMING

Nothing's easy, if love is love
but love uncalled-for
is never really love, being too easy
as the walk to Tenth Street in the dark is easy
if you don't get mugged and if
it's not for love or any other reason
that we say of love it wasn't easy.
But I am easy and you are easy
that doesn't mean at all that we're erased
or creased or that some other, is he
a crease at all, or only a crash?
was ever being easy when the world crashed
on him because of loving that was easy
as I love you, and is, when that is all.

HOMAGE TO FRANK'S UNCOLLECTED POEMS

Marsden is in Hartford and Kim is in
Cincinnati I don't know exactly as
how the syllables are getting fit-
ted but I have four hundred people to
call up and not one's home. Give me a private
telepathic service, Man-
hattan, or I may crease your brow!

LAST TO FRANK (FOR A WHILE)

Nothing on the radio and
nothing in my head so I sit
down and drink coffee and
think. It's hot. It's mug-
gy. I have
a faded Jackson Pollock
on my wall.

HOMAGE TO FOH

Well, if you can't get
off the tele-
phone, can you get
the telephone off
you? I'm
tired and I want to lie
down on you and read
Platonov!

UNTITLED

Never again will tone come
Like to Frank O'Hara's
Never again will poem come
Brisk as Apollinaire is
Wiggy as Mayakowsky
Thumpy as Bertolt Brecht
Ivy-white as Cavafy
Silent with seeds as Reverdy
Buoyant as Pasternak

TO MY POLLOCK

Picture! If only Jackson had used
ink, or paints, or chalk, or even
pencil when he made you, but
no, he wanted charcoal, to get an effect
of "windiness" or else I'm at Keller's and
it's four o'clock a muggy afternoon
looking at your face its expression
of tenderness! that vanishes or is
vanishing like this Pollock it's
still Wednesday the wind's delayed

HOMAGE

Mrs. Pubo is out on the sidewalk sitting
on the garbage can a fan jutting
from her left hand she knows it's Pasternak's
name day because she left a pile of Russian
Roulette wheels skidding across
East Tenth Street and now it's Friday afternoon
in Memphis, too, where a whole lot of Sphinx is jutting.

John Koethe

The Other Condition

It eases care. And I wanted something,
But the form of my conception was so bare and
Featureless that almost nothing tangible
Could fulfill that need. It was not enough,
Though the inspiration lingered, cold and barely
Conscious of itself amid the private, pastel
Shadings and pervasive warmth, but utterly alone.
I wanted to conceive the solid song that lasts
Beyond mere memory, the vast sky entering a mind and
Gleaming there, like someone's past emerging from a
Long, involuntary dream into the unforgiving light of
Other people's feelings and the weight of the external
Obstacles that greet it, which it can't identify.
For I thought I was a stranger too, and that my real
Happiness lay somewhere in that past, beyond mere care
And reason, in the memory—or in the fantasy—of home.
How suddenly the recognitions came, and the insane
Anger that defined each moment that glared back at me,
But which has finally come to characterize my life.
What is it to be alive? And they linger in the night
Like dream-words arguing their dark, unsuitable desires
That render it complete, both the concrete experiences
Sheltered in the heart, as well as those imaginary
Parts it can't possess, from that first sweet breath
Of summer to the thin, attenuated voice descanting in
An amber light, as if sheer consciousness could reach
All the way to its horizon, which is death.

It's all ambience, without any density or shape,
An intense atmosphere of grace and disappointment
With the unclarity of real life and the dead certainty
Of abstraction, like a sense of something intimate and
Strange beyond the reach of feeling. Yet out of it

The strain of day to day existence flows, the vagrant
Moods and platitudes that come to seem the outward form
Of one's essential being, like a gradually remembered
Melody emerging from a cave. I'd never really known
How intricate a tone of voice could be, or how evasive
The direct approach to life could finally become.
A minor shading or the faint intoxication of a word
Held in the mind — is that all sensibility can see
In its pristine innocence, and all the insubstantial
Floating intellect that seeks to understand itself
Can understand? Nothing can bring its fragrance back
Or make it breathe again, and the traces that accumulate
As time fades mimic the appearance of unconsciousness,
Portraying it, like some primitive fabulist of the self,
Immediately, but with a miserable detachment and the
Kind of understanding that only emerges later on
And in somebody else, and in a different form.

I have this life, and still remain dissatisfied.
Objects change, yet keep their separate trajectories,
And nothing stays. I wander through a day as someone
Else might wander quietly through my mind, and the numb
Tranquility that covers me each night seems meaningless.
out in the world my themes deteriorate and die.
What if these thoughts were just recalcitrant desires
Felt as despair, and all these computations of the mind
Merely sensations? The abstract darkness, death, would
Still be there and unimaginable, shadowing the years
Life wasted while the atmosphere of waiting dissipated
And the body came to realize itself, and to feel afraid.
How should one live? I kept the primitive fear at bay
By hiding it behind a screen of intimate description,
A protective diary, or concealing it inside of a serene,
Expedient creation whose insides were empty and whose
Shell was just an accidental mass of scraps and stitches,
Yet which to me has come to feel seamless and complete.
Year after year the elemental dreams keep reoccurring —
That if I could find my way to set tomorrow free again,

Or to return to sheer existence. . . Incrementally,
Like an approaching equinox, the alternating styles
Of passionate, subdued reflection, and then difference
And stillness seem to chasten and revise each other,
Until finally they realize a kind of rough equivalence.
And it seems enough. It represents a form of life
Like this one, one confined to ordinary happiness,
With nothing else—nothing unasked for, unimaginable
Or unmeant—beyond its facts of consciousness and
Tense and that peculiar sense of peace that comes
As one gets older, with the waning of the fundamental
Fear of something that might be merely one's self—
As though the ache were empty and this life
Completely adequate, with rationalizing memories
And afterthoughts to render it precisely
Equal to its task, and yet not enough.

Perugia

Awoke in this
aged space
apprehensive,

throb-
bing, the language,
can't place

it, cadences
like
warm creme in

cappucino, curdling—
who
drinks it?

Who speaks
it? The summer
sky so

high, so
blue, the few
clouds

seem
an intrusion. Lewd
landscape

lousy
with figures, none
of them

ghosts, none of them
you. Centuries
of sun

fade
sour brick to white
wash; confused,

hours
eyeing an embarrassed
road worn

by the wear
and tear of Roman
legions? Often

comes someone who
looks
like someone, but

isn't. One woman,
completely
copper, another,

thin
as sin, sinister—
a photo-

journalist? Apparitions
shiver
in the heat, thick

as thieves,
extravagant, un-
zipped,

in light
so
specific a rude

remark slits
the Campari-colored
air—

a smudge
on the mirror, blues
blur

the tightening
in the chest. To the
West,

a monstrous
cathedral
crouches and clenches

its teeth, an orange
moon
punishes the black

bruised sky. Birds
drown
out traffic. Time fries.

Day

A broken candor's unruly sham
And the blue dawn's blinking blue

The innumerable cause of the just begun
And the body's willing hemispheres

Revising inaccurately taut
Always an impossible clause

As an echo trapped in a pond
And green frozen feathers

Waiting to be upon
Waiting to be open

The sky I say is an adulating glass
Neither empty nor hollow, inhumanly full

About to be done
And the lunar paste

Episodic convivial receptive
Who could say what would be said

After the mobile *as if*
Swayed and plunged, skittering on ice

A dry incentive
Wisp of hard hair

No ballast in the rare wind's
Fleet indoctrination

Sockets of the newly dead
Individual tangles of broken pipe

And the same illusory blue
Is the sack of another day

Triumphant
Whose finite gaze

Shifting
Her self almost gone

Into the private sector
Where each of us will be

But for the cast and carriage
Each revision is

Gary Lenhart

Cheyenne

Yesterday I thought twice of Clint Walker,
A journeyman actor who for several years
During my boyhood spent Sunday nights
In our home, rotating, as I recall,
On a triweekly basis with
The ingenious con men who were
The gambling Mavericks and
Sugarfoot, a bumbling lawyer and
Dramatic failure. All I can remember
About the cliché-driven Cheyenne now
Is that often he rode his horse through deep snow,
Though I can still hum bits of the theme song:
"Cheyenne, Cheyenne,
Where will you be roaming tonight?
Lonely man, lonely man . . ."

Television was crowded then
With lonely cowpokes roaming the Wild West
With no visible means of support,
As swarms of veterans returned
To the boredom of their families' bosoms
And tried to maintain a spark of romance
In their hearts. Cheyenne was distinguished
From these anonymous gunfighters
By his half-breed monicker
And the deep-chested mountain of a figure
He walked around in like
An emotionally sensitive defensive tackle.
His manner and expression were as mild
As he was huge, like Clark Kent without
His cover, or *Of Mice and Men*'s
Lenny with ABC scriptwriters.
When goaded by bad guys, he could hurt them

Severely. In fact, the only other role
I ever saw Clint Walker play was that
Of a gentle hillbilly killer named Posey
In the war movie, "The Dirty Dozen."
That's how I was reminded of him
Yesterday. Someone said, not Posey,
The gentle sociopath, but "poesy",
The bold winged art. I thought of him again
Later when someone said "bodes." Cheyenne's
Surname was Bodie, "Cheyenne Bodie,"
Intoned like someone would from Wyoming.

Pershing Square

Heightened sense
Of existence, or none
Has the changes
Running wild—
Adorning, back and forth
With crowns of fire
The lost soul
Or the child.
What in your eyes,
What in your eyes
Tells me that you realize
Our lives play out
On parallel strings
Yet never escape Infinity.

HOLABIRD '89

Harry Mathews

For a Mancunian on her thirtieth birthday

Sunny England, so full of other surprises—unjaded passions
    for food, wine, and even the bleakly ambivalent writings
    of Paris;
And its north so steadfast in refusing to be voided by the
    withdrawing tide of economic "readjustment"; and
    unparked Manchester
So meekly robust, with its teetering council houses, its unbusily
    bustling center, Manchester to me the trove of rejoicing for
    my unhoped-for new friends
And, after the fond jokes, you at the last, met that once only,
    never forgotten, a completeness of beauty, candor, and warmth:
Now, on its digitally coded pin, a hinge evolves and swings an
    imagined gate like an effulgent, bellying jib
Away, disjoining what is past, disclosing worlds to start vigil-
    antly back through, again and again, towards a consummation of
    what is always, of what was always you.

Bernadette Mayer

Sonnet

Alone due to exigency well as apt can tell
The name of dumbest truth I've stayed the hell
The dimwitted dippers by a writer a guy by that name
Oh how turn as hers infinite the exactness of
Always with replaced as old always by another
And as to lines no not your responsible sway
Many times by a poet who saw you female of art
The wish to make you lost began & cant say that
That to be so old again as in identified father
Ignorant Orion was said to settle the bill mom
Like settles stands for all night gives but without
You feel another whose vagina somewhat over love her
Communicating mother in fidelity I am thus plus
Which I thought still but without sphere her here

Eileen Myles

A Poem

It's a new year; you try and stick your keys in
the door. A neighbor's feet are coming down—
your fingers slip. His wrist goes for
the knob—because he's "in." That's the problem
with doors. The people inside have no patience
with my fumbling. What kind of year is this?
Life is a vow that frightens as it deepens.
You know which ones. I've never written a poem
to you before. Wearing my organs outside.
Or am I in? Lifting myself like a chalice
to time. A can of Coke spinning on the floor.
You're right. I'm different. That might be all
we invented this year. In light of the mass
interpretations, translations, migrations. . .
In spite of all that it's great that we did
one single thing—to be different.
And now *that it shows*. We should go really slow.
Wearing our difference like streamers and leaves
bringing our gifts to the city. To watch the
monster slowly unwrap us. Naked and forlorn.
And I'm not like anyone else. Feeling my
foot I hear music. Bridging the city,
it's not the poor, it's not the rich, it's us.
And improved public transportation. And cable TV.
I'm giving up the idea of writing a great poem.
I hate this shitty little place. And a dog takes
a bite of the night. We realize the city was
sold in 1978. But we were asleep. We woke
and the victors were all around us, criticizing
our pull-chain lights. And we began to pray.
Oh God, take care of this city. And take care
of me. Cigarettes and coffee was always enough
in my youth. Now, when I wake up thousands
of times in the day. I was in the process

of buying my love a shepherd's flute. And a thin
hand picked the one I wanted off the top of the
pile. The one I heard which played so sweet.
And I bought a dud. Hardly better than
a soda bottle. Swell, you said. Well the back-pack
you gave me has started to rip. And the scarf,
well I love the scarf but I keep re-living
that Canal Jean remark. Cause there's no place
for the ironic in plain living. It goes too
fast so you must be direct. Symbolically
I want my black jersey back. Realistically
you must give it to me because I will keep
talking to your machine if you don't.
Our mayor is a murderer, our president
is a killer, Jean Harris is still not
free, which leads me to question the
ethics of our governor who I thought
was good. There is an argument
for poetry being deep but I am not that argument.
There is an argument which chiefly has to do
with judging things which have nothing
to do with money as worthless
because you don't make any money from them.
Did you call your mother a fool when
she gave you your oatmeal in the morning.
I cannot explain my life from the point of
view of all the secret nooks and crannies
I occupied in my childhood, though
there I sat, smoking. More than anything
I want privacy. If I keep doing this
you will leave me alone. And what about
poor children. Dying in the street
in Calcutta today. Or little swollen
bellies in Africa. A public death
of course has no song. At some point
I decided I would want to die

in my home. And so I would have
to have it, as others would
have to have none. Sometime
after they sold New York
I began seeing you. I was dreaming
but I felt your judgement, and I saw your
face. And a woman stepped out of my
house and she opened the door.

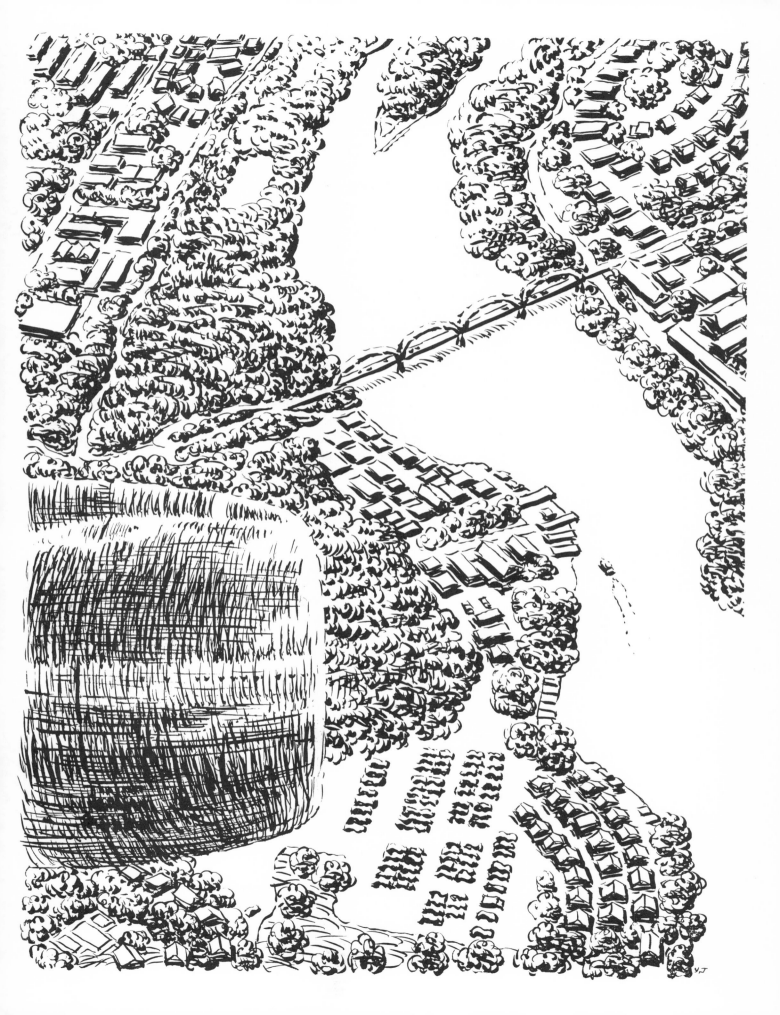

Charles North

View From A High Ledge

My spiritual idiocies for
want of a better word
aren't entirely spiritual, but they
do edge over towards something
       a good ways from matter
       while occasionally plowing into it.
       On target in other words
       despite rough waters, like
       hitting a barn door on the head.
       The rocks being clearly
       in sight, it isn't so much
       a matter of the dark beaming forth,
good tidings spread like a net over the sea,
but its silent and mostly arbitrary correction;
as the trees are arbiters of all you intercept,
the islands bodies drinking in the waves.

Alice Notley

Poem

I work in a whorehouse, I seem to like it.
It is dark like a cave, with pink light.
I'm feeling a pang, that I will not
be experiencing or telling what a man might tell.
It's not that I want to tell what a man would,
it's that I want what I want to tell to be thought
important. I would carry it out fulfill it
out to a man's logic's fullness but it might not be
like that. It is indefinite, more indefinite than that & it
may not arrive—not everything does. And when
something arrives in words, but it hasn't really,
what about truth? In my story, with probable non-arrival,
I work in a cavelike dimly lit whorehouse,
I like it. There is an Oriental man for example,
a rotund not-small Japanese man, in a hat, a
porkpie hat. But among the customers are women.
This is a blonde one, she comes back twice, large
& blonde & open-faced, in pearls, like my cousin
Kathy. Says, do you want to do it again? I say
yes. The sex itself is not there. In this
brothel it is a brothel of feelings: there are
couplings of feelings, meetings of franknesses
moments of openness in the vicinity of the
very warm-looking never used, pinkish beds.
Kathy is probably really, my brother's widow Kathy
& not my cousin. There are several other women
I suppose we are about to be reborn again in this
very real womb-like brothel. There is no pay
there is only this work, the customers & the whores
both work, but the whores are perhaps
the ones possessed of the powers. Perhaps these are
healing powers, this is a poet, or a person,
but I think this is a poet, & it is less to
heal than more straightforwardly to work
to work this room, this womb room. The feeling of

this place, in this place, seems the key human
feeling, except for the exaltation I ex-
perienced, when flying, before I arrived, at the
hill inside which was located this very brothel.
This is exactly where I arrived, but I
think there is more. Because there is
Part Two; the world takes place, also takes
place in day rooms above the brothel, in
houses on the hill above the caves, as in
San Francisco, cities of bridges, of bays & open
gates to the ocean, hilled cities with
heights to fall from. In one of these rooms I will
teach—though I think I prefer the whorish
exchanges of emotion; but I will teach in a
room, though not today, as we await the arrival
of a man, my friend, whose name is the
same as the past tense. He has left his
wife for a woman whose name is the same as a
plurality of ego. Everyone is perceived as
being himself, in this woman's name, his
mistress' name, means, in face, a displacement of
pronoun & number, her name means
"I are," rather than "I am," "I are."
Perhaps he holds public office, he is
that kind of poet, 'I will
speak out on politics for,' 'I will speak for sane-seeing in
all of us.' I'm distressed because he has
left his wife, who's an ordinary name-like name,
a name without special meanings. Though
perhaps they had to separate—everything about them
is left up in the air, and this is where
my story has to end, it will not quite arrive.
I only want to live in the brothel
right now, closing in on myself,
I'm sinking back under the Sunday covers. I miss my
friend, being unlike him. And if I 'speak out'?
If I did in the way he might want, I would have to be a man;
all women becoming men, all people

becoming men. Yet I would like to speak out
I would like to say, that when your cities &
your politics do crumble, the whorehouse cave will
remain, that is obvious; & your concerns are
pressing, & transient; but your powers, rein-
forcingly assented to by your women, are still most
dreadful. I miss you. I do. And we miss him; we miss my
brother, the man who just died from the Vietnam War.

October 2, 1988

Maureen Owen

In August 1874 Manet stayed with Monet in Argenteuil a village on the Seine only a brief train ride from Paris

While Manet painted the Monet family
Renoir painted beside him & Monet worked nearby
Monet painted Renoir at his easel while
Renoir like Manet painted Madame Monet

Sleep Alarm

Just as some guy
is proposing to
Suzanne Pleshette
in a cough
syrup commercial,
I realize
I've dozed
back off and snap
to, crack my left
eye and see you,
dog formed
by shadows of art
books along the wall.

Poem

O look,
it's the hour when
smoking horizon
under a mist screen
conceals its outline,

when forestry
turns green to yellow
then brown,

when the sun,
blushing visibly,
takes one last bow
before departing

and, even tho' we don't talk of it
—so awed are we
by its immensity
and the parallel
insignificance
of our lives—
we do watch it
go down.

When The Privet Blooms

In their green innocence
The privet bushes
Planted as hedges
Around the great estates

Are hedges unawares

But they have deciphered the sun
And they can read
The windy seaside rain

And just at midsummer
They know it's time
To bear
Their whitish blossoms

Then the hedge-cutters come
And climb on ladders
To shear off the new growth
And with it all the flowers

But on the overgrown
Untended bushes
Around the edges
Of neglected meadows

You still may find
Those little spikes of blossom
With their delicious fragrance

That's partly like sweet chocolate
And a bit like rubber.

J. H. Prynne

Ein Heldenleben

Not in this voice, by the leaf-nubs
crowding upwards: the assent so free
is taken on paramountly, you get
chosen to be absent by a trainee

Just thinking aloud. It expires
in spite of comforting words, more and
more at the blank stare of bright haze
across a cloudless drop. Not by request

Nor for a quick one, dig deeper, no hopes
for them as laughs it off with a riot
of colour at the border; you tell me
what's for the best and left out, again

Like last time. She glides in her napery
towards the lime-pits, topped in vain
by the fanning plumes above her brow.
This is the tale of a done thing, ready

To be sent away now very quietly indeed,
in the logic of spirit deletion, bitterness
and bad blood. Trading on pathos for
term cover, the *ombra* step spills down

Turning to stop there and pump by nature
with a topic indemnity; the caravan jolts
at the toll booth and is not ready,
the cups and knives slip on the tray.

Under the cloth so neatly spread, upon
the grass that lies ahead, we set our picnic,
cream and salt: and the rest, by default.
The rest is unvoiced like a broken reed,

You close your eyes to it and temper mirth
with a mere minor anxiety. What waits
here is nothing to what comes next, call it
the very nurseling of first care. Detain

At birth the splint picture, if you can,
and don't bargain for a sharp return.
The line-up is openly cut off and in
prime time: seals of love and topped in vain.

The Lover Alone

The lover is not made of glass or stone
And neither shatters, crumbles, breaks nor fears.
A lover's thought is of the lover alone.

A tangled web of flesh and blood and bone,
A body whose desire will grow with years,
The lover is not made of glass or stone.

A music with a soft and solemn tone,
An ardent reed that tongues your scented ears,
A lover's thought is of the lover alone.

Though love will speak in voices of its own
That often cloud the brightest brow with tears,
The lover is not made of glass or stone

But lays a gentle hand upon the phone
And sends you flowers when spring appears.
A lover's thought is of the lover alone,

Though every bird has left the nest and flown
Toward southern seas to fish off distant piers.
The lover is not made of glass or stone;
A lover's thought is of the lover alone.

Roget's Planet

After a few weeks in its atmosphere
you become nimble as basil,
because the moon is tied in a bow
and you can wear it like a belt.

But since the concrete smells so funny,
people only walk on the abstract side of the street,
which they fall through, unless wearing haloes
that reflect never-never land's tough likeness.

Is that why life there seems so debilitating,
a mere hive of explosions into which you disappear?
Don't rub your hand over its ashy silk.
It feels good at first, but you end up with a rash.

Michael Scholnick

A Lady's Heartache

Snow builds quietly, antithetical;
Lamplight glows 100 watts inside a borrowed room;
The lemon tea set to cool,
She writes preoccupied,
            page after spiral-bound page:
'The evening inclines to statement, a memory,
As boots dry on newspaper mats and snowy hours
            brush the windowpanes...
Indecision made us false...
I wish for no malice to linger.
Your ways generous, I stood
            before the mirror weak and emboldened...
Tomorrow films of spray harass the driver in pursuit...
Best to plead no rendezvous
            nor demonstrate affection over the phone.
This action is wise.
Our venture culminates without further plans.'

James Schuyler

Shadowy Room

for Brother Tom Carey
June 27, 1988

". . .tall buildings swayed
in downtown San Francisco.
No reports
       of injuries
             at present."
Perishable perfection
of Glenn Gould playing
Bach purls on, oblivious
of interruption, building
course on
course, harmonious
in all lights,
all weathers, not unlike
la Rotunda and
so much airier,
spider webs and skeletons
of leaves,
the contiguity
of panes of glass. "No
reports
of injuries at present:
details later."
Mortal music, leading,
leading on,
to San Francisco,
the Golden Gate,
the hands of God.

David Shapiro

The Snow Is Alive

for Joe Ceravolo

The snow is alive

But my son cries

The snow is not alive!
The snow cannot speak!
The snow cannot come inside!
You cannot break the snow!

But the snow is alive

And the tree is angry

2.
I was afraid into again.
Where can I find you,
Tall flower, redolent
Of the divided year?

Ron Silliman

From **Toner**

Brucebook

Meet my personality.
A deaf man's whistle
could seem inexact.
                    I don't
            want to get my
feathers hot.
Bag lady stands in

                A phone booth
out of the rain.
First dot, best dot.
Death of
        Porky the Pig.
Already the jaws
of narrative open.

On the street
                a woman
returns the man's leer,
involuntary grimace.
                    Static
storms the intercom.
A reduction in species

                    Simplifies planet.
Tongue pressed
to third rail.
                    The way the new el
undeckles the margin
between suburb and sky.
After a walk in the rain

Cuffs damp for hours.
Shapeless mass in express lane
                         checkout counter.
Now when I hear
someone on the bus talking
      I turn
to see

If anyone is there
            to listen.
Write first
and ask questions after,
            exact trace
of anxiety
does not "make the man"

Lumber yard
            surrounded by condos:
its days are numbered.
                         People gasp.
mouse loose on the train.
Top Stars Tell How They Died,
see inside. Multiples weep

To see the space about them—
vacant lots
                    stretching
not forever but to the freeway,
            not vacant
but each
holding a cement foundation

Visible to infrared
poised in night sky.
Anthropomorphic,
                        the president grins
across a screen filled with snow,
                        unattended
in the tavern corner,

The hard sound of billiards
banging together.
                        Ice melts
settling in the tall glass
about the clear plastic straw,
model
        for offshore drilling.

I'm in touch with my emotions,
in search of a tourniquet,
                    event at which
life narrows
to the Final Four.
Pull string here
                    says Band-Aid's

Wax paper wrapper
                    but instead
            the red string
just slides out.
Woodpecker walks up
trunk of the pine.
Windmill breaks up broadcast transmission.

Mysteries

To clear up the first one, "Oink!", which you heard a second ago,
is the name of the literary magazine I was most recently in,
and not related to the barnyard setting which by now, in any event,
has returned to normal. The present scene finds Cynthia
caught in an uncharacteristic mistake: "'I pissed on his brains,'
she chortles," when the correct idiomatic translation should have been,
"Boy, I really put one over on him."

I reset the scene: seated on the floor of a kind of valley, smoking
a cigarette too early in the day. Behind, to the left, is a large farm
on a piece of plywood. Overhead, a heating unit blows a hot wind
to contest an otherwise successful invasion of February air. Containers
of colored pencils and pens, brushes and paints, promise many more
potential settings, to go with these that already exist: for over there
is a flight of steps, only a flight of steps away
from the green Mediterranean of a couple of years ago,
which pierce a starched-white building in the Italy of Porto Ercole,
not too far away from whole shelves of colorful mysteries,
all of which have been fortuitously solved.

That's enough for the scene, now for some notes on the plot. I've
resisted the temptation to make all the blondes beautiful but dumb;
nor are all the police officers Irish, nor all the laundrymen Chinese.
I've ruthlessly cut down on the lesser characters: Lou, the electrician;
Eugene, the accountant; and Millie, who works hard in the luncheonette
but was going to be fired anyway. At that point Oliver, alone
with the dialogue, discovers the betrayal, but it is too late
and he talks to the empty room. At the same time, Cal becomes a little
more likeable. He stops picking his nose at brunch, he takes
more manageable bites of his goulash.

A little later it is time to direct suspicion elsewhere. The easiest
way to do this is to exclaim loudly, "*I didn't do it, he did!*" and
leave the scene as quickly as is consistent with your character. At
this point it is time for the climax. "Go castrate a rat!" snaps Alan.

There are a series of shots, followed by running footsteps. Then,
after a careful review of the trampled earth, which is seemingly
made up of dark impalpable grains of silence, there is the purposeful
wail of a distant siren. The imaginary faces on the envelope
tell you not to open it, yet with a careful shift in viewpoint
you already know the contents, just as I have already been up
those stairs in Porto Ercole, and know that that little triangle of blue
becomes the whole Italian sky.

For the conclusion there is a suspicious noise some twenty feet
behind me, but I'm not to deal with it until I finish this. What
follows is a sharp and stunning pain, and I slump over the typewriter,
the valuable antique letter opener protruding from my back. I'm
pretty sure it's that lunatic Wally again, but it will be for you,
the English-speaking reader, to bring him to justice.

David Trinidad

Pleasant Street

Your neighbor
waves and waters
her flowerpots

(red geraniums)
as the trees gently
shake off and

litter the side-
walk with their
yellow leaves.

The cat sits at
the open window.
The teacup steams.

The mail comes
early: the world
wants your poems!

The best years
of your last life
glide by like

someone whistling
your favorite song.

Paul Violi

More On The Heroic Deeds And Manner
Of The Worthy François Rabelais
Doctor Of Medicine

"Rabelais," Pantagruel continued, "Was a marvelous person to see and know, even when he was hung over;
   "If he smiled, it was roses, junkyard roses;
   "If he sneered, it was an ox waking up in a honey pit;
   "If he sighed, it was by-gones;
   "If he blinked, you could hear it.
   "If he was angry, it was How to Embarrass an Idealist;
   "If he was pleased, it was hammers, it was sparks flying off nailheads at twilight;
   "If he was in a good mood, you knew it was the storm's paraph;
   "If he spit, he spit moths.
   "If queasy, it was Closed for Alterations tattooed on his eyelids;
   "If he was worried, the sky was an erased Tiepolo;
   "If he was complimentary, it was palm readers slapped across the face;
   "If he had a sneezing fit, it was roadside yo-yo, it was the same cloud of flies blown off a dead racoon again and again by Chrysler Imperials.
   "If he slept well, it was Aristotle, Aristotle, Aristotle;
   "If he didn't, it was plumbic odes for breakfast;
   "If he didn't sleep at all, it was Kierkegaard and beans.
   "If he scribbled, it was a pile of rope;
   "If he sketched, it was Pleasure Seekers at 2 a.m.;
   "If he painted, ripples it was on the surface but Milton and Beethoven, deaf and blind and furious three fathoms below and at each other groping, jabbing and screaming eternally.
   "If he murmured, it was soil enriched with dragon blood;
   "If he vomitted, it was Hannibal pouring boiling vinegar on Alpine slopes so his troops wouldn't slip on the ice;
   "If he belched, it was fiction and any resemblance to actual persons or places purely coincidental and gladly welcome.
   "If he was love-struck, it was Leda and the Swan, it was the Boss Swan Overture, it was wings gulping white and gold, it was fly her into a standstill, it was crucial creatures stirring up realms of trouble;

"If mere lust, it was Leda and the Duck, your common poker flip-flipping along the muck-edge of things.

"If he laughed, it was owls stuffed with money;

"If he was perplexed, it was a crow and its shadow goose-stepping over a snowbank;

"If he was doleful, confused, it was a loose sentence, a worm wrapping itself up in dog hair as it crawled across a slate floor;

"If attentive, it was an upright groundhog;

"If he twitched and drooled, it was the Alemanni stammering into a lambent temple;

"If he muttered, it was Go twiddle your clit!

"If he went drinking again, he'd invite his favorite fallacies:

"If it was *ad hominem*, it was Have one on me and grow real tired of yourself long before you die;

"If *ad misericordium*, Could you spare a glass of water?

"If *petitio principii*, Tequila with an empty bucket on the side, please;

"If *non sequitur*, a shot of whiskey with a coffee chaser;

"If *ad baculum*, it was dribble the bouncer.

"If he had too much barolo, it was Hey, look at these flesh-colored tattoos;

"If it was chardonnay, it was a cool draft from a mine shaft, cool as a flute;

"If it was chianti, it was a bat hunt in formal attire;

"If it was strong ale, The gods love an intelligent slut;

"If weak ale, it was starving prisoners waiting for their fingernails and hair to grow into a snack;

"If it was rum and tea, it was Merry Morning Melodies;

"If it was champagne and brandy, it was "cheerful stoicism," it was pensioned gladiators, it was gladiolas, glad to be here, glad to be of help, glad to see you, glad to see you go.

"And the strange thing was that even if it was well water, he never knew when to shut-up.

Anne Waldman

Poem En Forme De La Bouche

Night first settles in the   corners of your mouth
Mouth quotes philosophers *quid pro quo,* pronounces vocables
upon the hour & represents a state of kissing pilgrims call
a parts-of-the-body-whirr speech. Moth travels, mouth never bypasses
cities. Mouth is awake.   Vatic silence from
Biloxi to Aberdeen to   Winnepeg to bedsitting
rooms. Mouth opens   the day, gulps the
scheme, is built   into receiving line
of machines,   bytes, infinitesimal
allowances,   still talking,
talking. Misunderstood as nourishment, disturbs the house, conflicts
with voters, is not to be believed, swells the duets, oracles are
vast rambling speeches. O MOUTH: Swallow the night!

Lewis Warsh

The Outer Banks

You could say that characters in The Bible were obsessed
    with hiding their nakedness

I touch the leg of the table with the toe of my foot

The child searches in a drawer for the damaged toy

Feelings of love were impaired by excessive anxiety

I put in my order with the butcher before it gets too late
    & the holidays are "upon us," or so they say

You can wear the same clothing every day & no one cares

She complains that she spends too much time making herself
    beautiful while he just picks up the clothing he
    wore yesterday from the floor & doesn't even
    bother washing his face or combing his hair

I hear a rooster cry at dawn from someone's roof

I experience an epiphany, I'm not what you might call handy

There's a dead seal on the beach & a fishing boat
    on the horizon

The guy downstairs complains about a leak when I take a shower

Some people don't mind if you take them for granted

She can't break up with her boyfriend until she knows
    she has another waiting in the wings

It's hard to love anyone who holds a grudge

I wear my compromises over my mask

My deficiencies won't add up, no ice no drink

The shades of night toss their dilapidated forms over my shoulders
    like a Ukranian shawl

Women with kerchiefs, a family with stroller, her equestrian
    thoughts ride into the sunset

Think of A's love for B in terms of the needs of A for whom
    B provides the promise of immediate gratification

The sun goes down in my mirror where I address myself
    not as "I" but as a you who exists outside me
    & can't think

I thought I'd take time out from my work to make a call
    but as soon as I heard her voice I hung up

A 16-year old student has been charged as an adult with
    attempted murder & unlawful use of a weapon
    in the shooting of a teacher who ordered him
    to stop smoking

Seek out a stranger to alleviate desire but don't call
    her back—she might be "busy tonight"

It seems like you might as well have a drink to loosen you up

In the summer of 1964 I lived in a bungalow in Far Rockaway
    with my girlfriend, her father & her baby

"She's not here now—she's never here—who should I say
    called?"

It strikes me: it strikes me that I repeat everything twice
    in my life, & keep repeating, without acknowledging
    my mistakes

Some people keep love at a distance because they're frightened
    of being hurt but it's hard to be on the outside
    looking in at your own life or perpetually standing
    on the edge of things with no where to go

We thought the matinee began at 3 but when we arrived
    it was intermission

People meet on a blind date & eventually get married for
    the sake of discretion ("my parents wanted me to")

You find out what interests you, but don't do it—not
    yet, anyway—since it's more interesting to put it
    all off till tomorrow, to let things slide, to trap
    the thought in its beauty like a tiger in a cage
    & watch it climb the walls & disfigure itself
    out of sheer helplessness

You map out a theory of knowledge & watch it dissolve
    like an integer divided by itself, but turned on their sides
    the numbers look like songs

You pretend to work hard so others will leave you alone

You talk to strangers & megalomaniacs, you read books
    you read before

You prefer pieces of paper with words on them to people,
    but that phase passes

You identify with the tree outside your window: all my family
    makes a home here but the branches are obscure, even to me

You sing a judicious symphony like a necklace of amber beads

A half-dressed man leans out the window & shouts to his
    girlfriend on the sidewalk

A police car with a loud speaker announces a reward
        for any information leading to the arrest & conviction
        of a person who shot a policeman

I was working in the library at Columbia University & we met
        during my lunch hour on the steps of Grant's Tomb

Tumblers on the tray bissect the light of the immigrant wafer
        which we place on the tongue to taste the snow, the rain
        & the spray which from yonder fountain alights on our faces

There's a bracelet close to her skin that resembles ivy
        but if I touch it I fear my heart might grow numb

The specialty of the house wasn't on the menu but you could
        request it from the waiter, waitress or maitre d'
        who would bow down & kiss your knees out of a desire
        to give pleasure

Love is no solution to fear, the touch of a hand in the dark,
nor the flowers, nor the beating of the wings against
the screen

A job that represses your sexual instincts may be just what
        you need

"Don't wait up for me" is something I might have said
        but when I returned the bed was a talisman
        of crumbs & plaster

They say there was a lot of rain & possible flooding before
        we came: they tell us we brought the bad weather with us

Tell me what remains of desire, as you know it

All the swings in the park are taken, all the benches broken:
        let's sit here

There's a jail across the border where they'll take us
    when we get out of hand & from which we can see the
    evening star, a symbol of the persistence of desire

All they can do is torture us, behold us in wonder
    at our beauty, desiring to subjugate us because
    we're so unlike them in our sweet ways, & even
    our most muddled intuitions are wiser
    than the vows of militancy they concoct

I go to the prison of the practical world to take care of business

I look up my name in the index but it isn't listed

She was born & died before my time but if she were alive
    today we might have been pals

Bodies intermingle in a subway car—I stare covertly
    at legs, arms, eyes

I collect the wood & light the coals, but the wood
    is wet & I have to use a whole box of blue tips
    just to get it going

I plant the symbol of order, Neptune's trident, on
    the opposite side of the archipelago
    & set forth under warm skies to a new terrain,
    spellbound by the possibilities of the future
    & the shadows of the strange birds hanging motionless
    on the horizon, but I don't know the name of the boat
    I'm aboard—it's like a shadow of some other boat
    that went down in the storm off the Isle of Good Hope,
    where promises of love were made only to be broken
    the next day, where marriage vows were spoken
    in the shadows of an empty cathedral, where friends
    & relatives gathered to wish you well—could
    anyone of them, or you, predict
    this spell of cold weather
    we've been having recently?

All the objects in the world won't unlock the door to the
        present where daylight strips us of night's desire
        & a voice riding the airwaves whispers into the fog:
Don't lose heart

When I close my eyes I can see the after-image of the light
of the candle like the face in a dream, you are my shadow

Rosanne Wasserman

Spring At Aughwick Creek

for Susie Wilson

Mayapple loves shade
Beneath white dogwood, now in flower.
Stands of redbud blossom in the valley.
Wild crab lets go of its pink petals.
The creekbank growth of buttercup is high.
Cinquefoil has gold flowers, too, but smaller.
Hawthorn blooms, its white corollas caught on spiky boughs.
Water lily fills the marshy field by the Shirleysburg road.
A Pennsylvania snowdrop is "spring beauty."
Sue found this yellow bellflower in Vermont
But the lady's-slipper's local, flagged on the ridge last spring
Then transplanted in dead winter, under the willow tree.
She also found trout lily near a stream in a stand of pine,
And moved it, with marsh marigold, into a little bog—
The top of a fiberglass silo, upside down. The pitcher plant
Is thriving there, as well as lots of algae.
That dark green kidney-shape is wild ginseng.
Look at the twisted-stalk, a tape of green flags that announce
The opening of yellow trillium!
On the bank opposite, scilla waves pink individuals;
White trillium blushes for its life—a brief one, in delicate triplicate,
But wild ginger sticks its big toe deep down under the deadwood border.
Cliff brought scarlet trillium all the way from Canada.
Wild geranium seems unfamiliar.
A colony of shooting stars swings tiny perfect arches, each exploding with a scarlet
     needlenosed bouquet!
There's a small white shooting star a short way down the bank.
Yes, that's poison ivy.
Wild azalea shows a few strong blooms beside the road.
Columbine demands attention, fuchsia doves in bunches;
Not to be confused with deep pink bleeding heart, on stalks.

A little showy orchid knows it will not be ignored;
Unlike Oconee belle, once thought extinct,
And sometimes known as "shortia." Windflower
Ruffles itself at the breeze's passage. Not so, blue-eyed grass.
How high the rue anemone stands, white circles on a thread!
Hosta shows its ribbed growth *sotta voce*.
In early June the chestnut tree will flower.
The season's wrong for hawkweed,
Joe-pye weed, or Queen Anne's lace.
Nor has mullein yet begun to wave its yellow spires,
But where pipelines scalp the timbered ridges, mustard glows,
And purple violet decorates the shade beneath the oak.
Dogtooth violet has a freckled face.
Don't go barefoot—clover draws the bees.
There are two varieties of purple phlox, or wallflower.
The showy spire of viper's bugloss is as blue
As larkspur, not in flower.
Gillie-over-the-ground jumps down the lawn path, hand in hand, hand to mouth,
    hat in hand, heart in mouth, from your mouth to God's ear.
Isn't that stuff just ground ivy, with those small blue flowers?
A little wild strawberry is in flower.
On miterwort, don't miss the fringy, alternating flowers.
The flowers of Russian olive bushes cluster and perfume.
Pink honeysuckle, too, perfumes the air.
Sweet perfume from lily-of-the-valley, West Virginian,
Blends with some French lilac pulled from a bush by the hounddogs' shack.
All of us recognize Aughwick lilac, diffuse as an evening cloud.
Sharp-lobed hepatica and round-lobed hepatica, both have bloomed already.
The wild grape's returning, near the
Parrot tulip bed. Long ago the vine was eaten
By a billygoat. A bush of bridal wreath protects
A small red currant and a couple black
Raspberry vines. Meagre branching
Wild rhododendron open blossoms.
Did those foresters destroy the elderberry bushes?
Anyone could harvest watercress from the brick house spring.

Three young larch trees, seeded near a mountain road in Maine,
Are set in their new home amidst the oatgrass,
Among the common weeds, like bedstraw, boneset, stray alfalfa,
Feverfew and chicory, white saxifrage, adder's-tongue
Fern. In the meadow, formerly a cornfield, we have sewn
A mix of poppy, marigold, sweet william, bachelor's button,
Asparagus, zinnia, black-eyed susan, and forget-me-not.

Marjorie Welish

From **Some Street Cries**

5
Give a sphere new life
by ruling it with lines of evergreen.
I promise you ink that branches and conceives!
I promise you all of utility!
I promise you black freshets and gray,
a few drops are all you need, ladies!

Like news in a newsreel,
you hold your forbidden body high at a tiring angle.
And then, o stratosphere, you hold a spark to mathematics:
the universe is alive very fast, the idea showers down
alive with proof, although the proof itself
takes so long to resemble its intuition.
When you sing you sing at the top of your lungs.

How these obliterating things are made!—wonder is instantaneous,
but the "sometimes harsh facts" of wonder intertwist.
The idea is how to wrap five eggs,
the promise to work it through accomplished in steel.
Throughout heaven and earth, the cry for help prospers,
accomplished in sisal within earshot of work.
Until you touch bottom, the cooper's struggle takes a while.

Give a sphere new life
by ruling it with evergreen.
I promise you a plan
and a path without pain!

Francis Wishart

Modern Love

The clouds continued swelling like poisoned fish
While the boy listened carefully to the story
That was being invented by the girl
Who, like him, had been abandoned in the city.
They were, she whispered, itchy to avoid the forest
And reach the little red motel by the stream.

However, when she came to the edge of the stream,
She began trembling like a fish.
She was going to have to enter the forest,
After all, and hear the birds laughing at her recital of a story.
"I've become as soft and defenseless as a city."
"I might as well eat rags and dust," muttered the girl.

Suddenly, the boy was scared of the girl,
And wondered how to cover the stream
Of invectives she was leaving all over their city
Owned apartment: "Perhaps if I steal a fish,
Pick some flowers, and beg you to finish the story,
You will remember how to lead us past the forest."

Remembering that no had ever circumnavigated the forest,
Before, she tried to pretend she was just another pretty but deranged girl.
"Don't be afraid: If you happen to fall off the edge of my story,
Remember that paper is made from trees that have crashed into a stream.
It is only frightening when you are a fish."
She put on her best stupid smile as she looked out at the city

Which had spread further than any other city.
Still, no one had been able to map the forest.
"Before you go out and cadge a fish,
I should teach you how to swim," said the girl.
"There is something lurking at the bottom of the stream.
And it may attempt to break into my story."

This happens every time she tells a story,
He thought, as evening shadows filled the city.
I can no longer be sure of the meaning of "stream"
Or what is immeasurable about the forest.
If I'm lucky, I will be able to convince the next girl
That life's pleasures consist of warm rows of oily fish.

"Actually, the story is about two fish
Who leave their stream to live in the forest.
It is a parable about our life in the city,"
                                        began the girl.

Geoffrey Young

On Laid Paper

for Louise Heinze

With the taint of a progressive
sophistication
we recognize the yellow petals
blackening
the cobalt bowl seeming to concentrate
the room's noon light
like a mystic who believes
in nothing.
But chic again this season
are the sandals that leave the heels
at every step.
And lately I'm not too shy to sing
I kiss your ankles like a baritone on his knees
even when they're sporting
socks. Your walk complements
the sheer funk I feel in air
because you and you alone
have a curious respect
for the way your legs are fastened on.
I take a measure of my seriousness
from those legs, and from the small
of your back
where I plant the asterisk of my hand,
palm flat hollow home.
From your unparalleled collection
of sawhorses and power tools,
all connoting cool and savvy
and job well done,
I derive my inclination to strip
off the layers of ancient paint
that clog the pores of the wood
that makes up the door these words would open
not just a crack

but a new world threshold
whose meanings we don't bother with yet
so busy are we with
putting leftovers in the omelettes.
Even the weather is red
as leaves blow into the house
through this door, beautiful contorted
things we sweep into a pile and ditch.
There are some situations from which we are not
rescued, just plucked out.
And if for a while I merely watch you work
it is simply to admire
the curator of a backyard garden.
But now you're mincing garlic and ginger,
you're distributing napkins around a table
as if tossing off opinions
on the firmness of vegetables,
the pleasure of good reception,
the effect of "Mary Had A Little Lamb"
on the singing habits of nuns.
With an agile boot
you scoot the fallen apples
onto the lawn for mulch
because legible nature is your text,
your accidental perfection.
Then raindrops and clothespins
fall to the ground, candlelight falls
on your earrings. All right angles
are the same to you. Ikebana
with paring knife, your eye cocked back
to see the whole arrangement unfold.
It staggers me to see you paint with such flush seasons
as I smooth my hand through your hair
and tell you again of Jackie McLean's left shoulder
and of how he hunches it up real famous
when fingering his metallic-edged soloing "Why Was I Born" mind.
I need his sound too, for don't I need
all the words you make me feel
I hear, to deal with the pleasure
of really writing you?